QUIZ 1	6
QUIZ 2	8
QUIZ 3	10
QUIZ 4	12
QUIZ 5	14
QUIZ 6	16
QUIZ 7	18
QUIZ 8	20
QUIZ 9	22
QUIZ 10	24
QUIZ 11	26
QUIZ 12	28
QUIZ 13	30
QUIZ 14	32
QUIZ 15	34

QUIZ 16	36
QUIZ 17	38
QUIZ 18	40
QUIZ 19	42
QUIZ 20	44
QUIZ 21	46
QUIZ 22	48
QUIZ 23	50
QUIZ 24	52
QUIZ 25	54
QUIZ 26	56
QUIZ 27	58
QUIZ 28	60
QUIZ 29	62
QUIZ 30	64
QUIZ 31	66
QUIZ 32	68

QUIZ 33	70
QUIZ 34	72
QUIZ 35	74
QUIZ 36	76
QUIZ 37	78
QUIZ 38	80
QUIZ 39	82
QUIZ 40	84
QUIZ 41	86
QUIZ 42	88
QUIZ 43	90
QUIZ 44	92
QUIZ 45	94
QUIZ 46	96
QUIZ 47	98
QUIZ 48	100
QUIZ 49	102

QUIZ 50 104

QUIZ 51 106

QUIZ 52 108

QUIZ 53 110

QUIZ 54 112

QUIZ 55 114

QUIZ 56 116

QUIZ 57 118

QUIZ 58 120

QUIZ 59 122

QUIZ 60 124

QUIZ 61 126

QUIZ 62 128

QUIZ 63 130

QUIZ 64 132

QUIZ 65 134

QUIZ 66 136

QUIZ 67 138

QUIZ 68 140

QUIZ 69 142

QUIZ 70 144

QUIZ 71 146

QUIZ 72 148

QUIZ 73 150

QUIZ 74 152

QUIZ 75 154

QUIZ 76 156

QUIZ 1

1. Who taught Taylor Swift how to play three chords on guitar when she was 12?
2. What is the title of the poem that Taylor Swift wrote during her fourth grade that won a national poetry contest?
3. What year was Taylor born?
4. What is Taylor's middle name?
5. Who does Taylor consider to be her biggest influence?
6. If Taylor wasn't a singer, what has she said she would do as a career?
7. What high school did Taylor attend in Nashville?
8. What was the name of Taylor Swift's first album?
9. Which bank did Taylor sign up for a multi-year partnership with in 2019?
10. What is Taylor's star sign?

ANSWERS QUIZ 1

1. A Computer Repairman And Local Musician, Ronnie Cremer
2. 'Monster In My Closet'
3. 1989
4. Alison
5. Shania Twain
6. A Novel Writer, Interior Designer, Neurologist Or Psychologist.
7. Henderson High School
8. Taylor Swift
9. Capital One
10. Sagittarius

QUIZ 2

1. What is Taylor's brother's name?
2. How old was Taylor when she moved to Nashville?
3. What was the first song Taylor wrote?
4. Where was Taylor born?
5. Who inspired Taylor to become a singer?
6. Who is Taylor's BFF from high school?
7. How old was Taylor when she signed a publishing deal with Sony/ATV Music?
8. What is Taylor's shoe size?
9. What was Taylor's grade point average in high school?
10. How tall is Taylor?

ANSWERS QUIZ 2

1. Austen
2. Fourteen
3. So Happy
4. Reading, Pennsylvania
5. Marjorie Finlay, Her Maternal Grandmother Who Is A Professional Opera Singer.
6. Abigail Anderson
7. Fourteen
8. 8.5 Us
9. 4.0
10. 5'11"

QUIZ 3

1. What instruments does Taylor play?
2. What was the first thing Taylor did when turned 18?
3. How old was Taylor when she first kissed a boy?
4. What type of bug did Taylor have to knock off Christmas trees when she was younger?
5. What time of day was Taylor born?
6. Taylor loves Disney movies — true or false?
7. What type of bug is Taylor scared of?
8. Taylor has won the Album of the Year award at the Grammy's twice. Which albums won?
9. What was the first single Taylor released from her Lover album?
10. Which of Taylor's music videos won Video of the Year at the 2019 MTV Video Music Awards?

ANSWERS QUIZ 3

1. Guitar, Banjo, Ukulele And Piano
2. Registered To Vote — Online And In Her Pajamas.
3. Fifteen
4. Praying Mantis
5. 8:36 Am
6. True
7. Beetles
8. 1989 And Fearless
9. Me!
10. You Need To Calm Down

QUIZ 4

1. How many Billboard Music Awards has Taylor won?
2. How many copies of Taylor's album Lover were sold in the first week of release?
3. How many Grammy Awards has Taylor won?
4. What was Taylor's first single?
5. Taylor voiced which character in The Lorax?
6. What is Taylor's best-selling single so far?
7. What two songs has Taylor written for children with cancer?
8. What song has Taylor said is her favorite she's written and performed?
9. What is the name of the song Taylor wrote for Miley Cyrus?
10. Why did Taylor call her album Fearless?

ANSWERS QUIZ 4

1. 23
2. 679,000
3. Ten
4. Tim Mcgraw In 2006
5. Audrey
6. Shake It Off
7. The Unreleased 'Gracie' And The Charity Single 'Ronan'
8. Love Story
9. You'Ll Always Find Your Way Back Home
10. Because Tim Mcgraw Called Her 'Fearless'

QUIZ 5

1. What song won't Taylor perform because it makes her cry?
2. What song did Taylor write when she found out her friend was battling bulimia?
3. In which years did Time magazine name Taylor as one of the world's most influential people?
4. What are Taylor's seven studio albums?
5. What are Taylor's favorite songs to sing in karaoke?
6. Which mega-celebrity described Taylor as a "great writer"?
7. Where did Taylor perform her first concert on her Reputation tour in May 2018?
8. What date did Taylor release her album Lover?
9. What song did Taylor write as a last minute addition to Fearless after she broke up with Joe Jonas?
10. What is the name of Taylor's fragrance that comes in a music box?

ANSWERS QUIZ 5

1. Never Grow Up
2. Tied Together With A Smile
3. 2010, 2015 And 2019
4. Taylor Swift, Speak Now, Fearless, Red, 1989, Reputation And Lover
5. Grease Songs, Shania Twain And Dixie Chix
6. Neil Young
7. Glendale, Arizona
8. August 23, 2019
9. Forever And Always
10. Made Of Starlight

QUIZ 6

1. What fake name was used to hide Taylor's collaboration with Calvin Harris on This is What you Came For?
2. What two songs did Taylor perform with Paul McCartney at the Saturday Night Live 40th Anniversary Special after party?
3. What song did Taylor perform with Nicki Minaj at the 2015 VMAs, despite their feud?
4. As of June 2019, how much was Taylor estimated to be worth?
5. What was Taylor's first number 1 single on the US Billboard charts?
6. Who did Taylor write We are Never Ever Getting Back Together about?
7. Can you name three songs Taylor wrote about Harry Styles?
8. What record did Taylor break when she first appeared on Saturday Night Live?
9. For what song did Taylor win the 2019 MTV Video Music Award for "Best Visual Effects"?
10. How many Country Music Awards has Taylor won?

ANSWERS QUIZ 6

1. Nils Sjöberg
2. I Saw Her Standing There & Shake It Off
3. Bad Blood
4. $360 Million
5. We Are Never Ever Getting Back Together
6. Jake Gyllenhaal
7. Out Of The Woods, Style And I Knew You Were Trouble
8. She Was The First Ever Saturday Night Live Host To Write Their Own Monologue
9. Me!
10. Six

QUIZ 7

1. When was Taylor first seen in public with Joe Alwyn?
2. Who do people think Taylor write her song We are never ever getting back together about?
3. Which political heir did Taylor date in 2012?
4. Who broke up with Taylor over the phone in about 27 seconds?
5. How many kids has Taylor said she wants?
6. What blood type is Taylor?
7. Which long-haired musician did Taylor have a crush on, and wanted to marry, when she was younger?
8. How many houses does Taylor own?
9. Who was Taylor's Victoria's Secret model BFF, but they have since grown apart?
10. What are Taylor's Twitter and Instagram handles?

ANSWERS QUIZ 7

1. May 2016 At The Met Gala
2. Jake Gyllenhaal
3. Conor Kennedy
4. Joe Jonas
5. 10. 'Like An Army Of Kids,' She Said
6. Type O+
7. Taylor Hanson
8. Seven. 1 In Beverly Hills, 2 In Nashville, 3 In Nyc & 1 In Rhode Island
9. Karlie Kloss
10. @Taylor_Swift (Twitter)
    @Taylorswift (Instagram)

QUIZ 8

1. What two global airlines did Taylor partner with during her Red Tour?
2. What are Taylor's parents' names?
3. Which singer/songwriter did Taylor's parents name her after?
4. What was the name of Taylor's exboyfriend who she wrote Tim McGraw for?
5. What song did Taylor write for a boy she was in love with but he only saw her as a friend?
6. What nickname was given to Taylor by the media while she was dating Taylor Lautner?
7. How much money did Taylor donate to the Tennessee Equality Project in 2019?
8. Who is Taylor currently dating (Oct 2019)?
9. What did Taylor do the day before her Reputation tour started?
10. How long did she date Tom Hiddleston for?

ANSWERS QUIZ 8

1. Qantas And Air Asia
2. Scott And Andrea
3. Taylor
4. Brandon Borello
5. Teardrops On My Guitar
6. Taylor Squared
7. $113,000
8. Tom Hiddleston
9. She Invited 2,000 Foster And Adopted Children To A Dress Rehearsal
10. Three Months

QUIZ 9

1. What is Taylor's lucky number?
2. How many songs has Taylor recorded that she wrote entirely by herself?
3. What are some of Taylor's favorite TV shows?
4. What did Taylor say were her favorite lyrics from her Lover album?
5. Who is Taylor's favorite author?
6. What does Taylor always have in her fridge?
7. How does Taylor like her sushi?
8. What are the color of Taylor's eyes?
9. What is one of Taylor's favorite cooking shows?
10. Who is Taylor's favorite actress?

ANSWERS QUIZ 9

1. 13
2. 50
3. Downton Abbey, Killing Eve And Queer Eye For A Straight Guy
4. "Our Songs, Our Films, United We Stand/Our Country, Guess It Was A Lawless Land/Quiet My Fears With The Touch Of Your Hand/Paper Cut Stains From Our Paper-Thin Plans."
5. Suzanne Collins
6. Hummus
7. She Eats It With Soy Paper Instead Of Seaweed.
8. Electric Blue With A Black Tint On The Outline
9. Barefoot Contessa
10. Jennifer Lawrence

QUIZ 10

1. What hospital was Taylor born in?
2. What breed is Taylor's cat Meredith?
3. Does Taylor have any tattoos?
4. What is Taylor's favorite drink?
5. At what event did Taylor sing the national anthem when she was 11?
6. How many awards has Taylor won since starting her career? (Oct. 2019)
7. Where did Taylor first meet Britney Spears, of whom she is a massive fan?
8. What are Taylor's nicknames?
9. What is the name of the Taylor's first fragrance?
10. What song did Taylor sing to win a talent show when she was 11?

ANSWERS QUIZ 10

1. Bramptom Civic Hospital, Room 18
2. Scottish Fold
3. No. She Said She Doesn'T Think She Could Ever Commit To Any One Saying Or Symbol For The Rest Of Her Life
4. Diet Coke
5. Philadelphia 76Ers NBA Game
6. 337!
7. Britney Spears' Performing Arts Camp In 2003
8. Tay, T-Swizzle, Swifty, T-Swift & T-Sweezy
9. Wonderstruck
10. Leanne Rimes' Big Deal

QUIZ 11

1. What type of farm did Taylor grow up on when she lived in Pennsylvania?
2. How many Golden Globe nominations has she had?
3. What is the name of her character in the new Cats movie?
4. How did Taylor get a scar on her knee?
5. What is Taylor's favorite meal when she is in Nashville?
6. How does Taylor hold a pen when she writes?
7. Which fellow singer did Taylor write Bad Blood about?
8. What was the last stop on Taylor's incredible Reputation tour?
9. How many Teen Choice Awards has Taylor won (as of October 2019)?
10. In which movie did Taylor make her feature film acting debut?

ANSWERS QUIZ 11

1. A Christmas Tree Farm
2. Two
3. Bombalurina
4. From A Hot Glue Gun
5. Sweet Potato Pancakes From Pancake Pantry
6. She Places The Pen In Between Her Index And Middle Finger
7. Katy Perry
8. Tokyo, Japan
9. 26
10. Valentine'S Day, In 2010

QUIZ 12

1. What song did Taylor write for her mom as a Christmas present?
2. Which mega company did Taylor successfully complain to about receiving music royalties from?
3. On what date was Taylor Alison Swift born?
4. Taylor was raised for a time in Wyomissing, Pennsylvania, but she moved to Nashville Tennessee to pursue a career in country music at what tender young age?
5. When she signed with the independent label Big Machine Records she became the what?
6. What did Taylor Swift receive at the 2008 Grammy Awards?
7. How old was Taylor when her mother first put her in a saddle on a horse?
8. Swift's second album, Fearless, was released in what year?
9. At what age did Taylor win a local talent competition by singing a rendition of LeAnn Rimes's "Big Deal"?
10. Taylor Swift is the youngest person ever to be honored with what title?

ANSWERS QUIZ 12

1. The Best Day
2. Apple
3. December 13, 1989.
4. At the age of 14.
5. Youngest songwriter ever hired by the Sony/ATV Music publishing house.
6. A Best New Artist nomination.
7. Nine months.
8. 2008
9. Eleven.
10. Nashville Songwriters Association's Songwriter/Artist of the Year.

QUIZ 13

1. She spent her early years on a what in Cumru Township, Pennsylvania?
2. Which album became the best-selling album of 2009 in the US?
3. Taylor Swift's younger brother, Austin, is a graduate of what University?
4. The album Fearless won how many Grammy Awards?
5. How many copies of Swift's third album, 2010's Speak Now, sold within the first week of its US release?
6. Speak Now's third single, "Mean", won how many Grammy Awards?
7. Taylor Swift went on her first headlining tour in support of what album?
8. When she was nine, what did Taylor become interested in?
9. What was the name of Swift's her fourth album, released in 2012, which sold over one million copies in its first week of US release?
10. What song made Taylor the youngest artist to both write and sing a number one country song?

ANSWERS QUIZ 13

1. Christmas tree farm.
2. Fearless.
3. University of Notre Dame.
4. Four.
5. Over a million copies.
6. Two.
7. Fearless.
8. Musical theatre.
9. Red.
10. Our Song

QUIZ 14

1. Taylor Swift's singles "Shake It Off" and "Blank Space" reached how high on the Billboard Hot 100?
2. The Nashville Songwriters Association and the Songwriters Hall of Fame have honored Taylor as a what?
3. Swift's achievements include seven Grammy Awards, eleven Country Music Association Awards, twelve Billboard Music Awards, and how many Academy of Country Music Awards?
4. Swift has appeared as an actress in what comedy?
5. Taylor was in what two animated films?
6. Where was Taylor Alison Swift born?
7. In Swift's third studio album, Speak Now, all fourteen songs were written by who?
8. What does Taylor's father do for a living?
9. Taylor and her brother were raised in the Presbyterian faith and attended what?
10. Where did Taylor go to preschool and kindergarten?

ANSWERS QUIZ 14

1. Number one.
2. Songwriter.
3. Seven.
4. Valentine's Day (2010).
5. The Lorax (2012) and The Giver (2014).
6. Reading, Pennsylvania.
7. Taylor alone.
8. He is a Merrill Lynch financial adviser.
9. Bible school.
10. At the Alvernia Montessori School.

QUIZ 15

1. Where did the family move to when Swift was nine years old?
2. What was Taylor Swift's first hobby?
3. At the age of twelve Taylor was shown by a computer repairman how to do what?
4. In 2004, Taylor signed an artist development deal with what record company?
5. In 2004, Taylor became the youngest "what" ever hired by the Sony/ATV Tree publishing house?
6. What did Taylor Swift do for radio station programmers who played her music?
7. In late 2006, what country group did she opened for on the final nine dates of their Me & My Gang Tour?
8. In 2007, Taylor served as the opening act on twenty dates for whose tour?
9. Taylor Swift and Alan Jackson were jointly named the Nashville Songwriters Association's Songwriter/Artist of the Year in what year?
10. The lead single from Taylors album, "Love Story", was released in September 2008 and became the second best-selling country single of all time, peaking at what number on the Billboard Hot 100 chart?

ANSWERS QUIZ 15

1. Wyomissing, Pennsylvania.
2. English horse riding.
3. Play three chords on a guitar.
4. RCA Records.
5. Songwriter.
6. Baked cookies and painted canvases as gifts.
7. Rascal Flatts.
8. George Strait.
9. 2007
10. Four.

QUIZ 16

1. Who did Swift sing her song "Fifteen" with at the 51st Grammy Awards?
2. Taylor co-wrote and recorded "Best Days of Your Life" with what other female vocalist?
3. Taylor was the first country music artist to win an MTV Video Music Award when her song "You Belong with Me" was named Best Female Video in what year?
4. Who interrupted Taylor Swift's acceptance speech at the MTV Video Music Awards?
5. In 2010, Swift won four Grammy Awards from a total of how many nominations?
6. Swift became the youngest artist ever to be named "what" by the Country Music Association?
7. Speak Now was a major commercial success, debuting at what number on the US Billboard 200 chart?
8. Speak Now's opening sales of 1,047,000 copies made it the sixteenth album in US history to sell how many copies in a single week?
9. "As of February 2012, Speak Now has sold over 5.7 million copies worldwide. Taylor was named Entertainer of the Year by the Academy of Country Music in what two consecutive years?"
10. What organization named Swift 2011's Woman of the Year?

ANSWERS QUIZ 16

1. Miley Cyrus.
2. Kellie Pickler.
3. 2009
4. Kanye West.
5. Eight.
6. Entertainer of the Year.
7. number one.
8. One million.
9. 2011 and 2012.
10. Billboard.

QUIZ 17

1. You should take it as a compliment/ that I got drunk/ and made fun of the way you talk These lines are the first lines from which song?
2. It was the best of times, the worst of crimes, I struck a match and blew your mind, but I didn't mean it, and you didn't see it. What song is it?
3. From "Picture to Burn": "I realize you love _____ more than you could ever love me." What word(s) fills in the blank correctly?
4. This is the last time I'm asking you this, Put my name at the top of your list, This is the last time I'm asking you why, You break my heart in the blink of an eye, eye, eye These lines are taken from the song "The Last Time". Which singer collaborated with Swift on this single?
5. Dangerous What song is this, in other words?
6. Which song contains the lyrics "His voice is a familiar sound, nothing lasts forever"?
7. People like you always want back the love they pushed aside, but people like me are gone forever when you say goodbye. What song is it?
8. How old was Taylor when she met Abigail?
9. Finish this line; "You with your words like _____"
10. What comes next? "Love is a ruthless game, unless you play it..."

ANSWERS QUIZ 17

1. Gorgeous
2. Getaway Car
3. yourself
4. Gary Lightbody
5. Treacherous
6. Wildest Dreams
7. All You Had To Do Was Stay
8. Fifteen
9. Knives and swords
10. Good and right

QUIZ 18

1. From "Tim McGraw": "When you think happiness, I hope you think that little ___ dress." What color goes in the blank?
2. Which of these songs does NOT mention dancing?
3. Fill in the blank: "I'm walking _____ through the traffic light."
4. What is the first name of the high school crush mentioned in the first line (and indeed throughout the entirety) of "Teardrops On My Guitar"?
5. Kiss me, try to fix it, could you just try to listen? hang up, give up and for the life of us we can't get back. What song is it?
6. How old does Taylor Swift say you are "When somebody tells you they love you you're gonna believe them"?
7. What song are these lyrics from? "There's something about the way the street looks when it just rained"
8. What song do these lyrics come from? "You were in college, working part time waiting tables."
9. Where was Taylor Swift born?
10. What song is this line from? "Say you're sorry, that face of an angel comes out just when you need it to. . ."

ANSWERS QUIZ 18

1. black
2. The Story of Us
3. fast
4. Drew
5. Sad Beautiful Tragic
6. Fifteen
7. Fearless
8. Mine
9. Pennsylvania
10. White Horse

QUIZ 19

1. What song does this lyric belong to? "Once upon a time, I believe it was a Tuesday when I caught your eye"?
2. From "Dear John": "The girl in _____  cried the whole way home". What word(s) goes in the blank?
3. From "The Best Day": "I'm ___ years old It's getting cold I've got my big coat on." Which of these numbers fills in the blank?
4. Name the song that this lyric belongs to: "Now go stand in the corner and think about what you did!"
5. Final Sign of Affection?
6. Oh yeah, all right, take it easy baby, make it last all night. This lyric is from which song?
7. Finish this lyric: 'She looks at life like it's a party and she's ___'.
8. 'Just a boy in Chevy truck, who had a tendency of getting stuck on back roads'. Which song is this?
9. Finish this lyric: 'All this time I was ___'.
10. The first song released from Taylor's album "Speak Now" was "Mine". Finish the lyrics: "Do you remember we were sitting there by the ___"?

ANSWERS QUIZ 19

1. Forever and Always
2. the dress
3. five
4. Better Than Revenge
5. Last Kiss
6. American Girl
7. on the list
8. Tim McGraw
9. wasting, hoping you would come around
10. water

QUIZ 20

1. This song has the same title as one of Nicolas Sparks' books and a movie starring Channing Tatum and Amanda Seyfried. It is about the hurt and pain of a young girl who is abandoned, stranded and broken-hearted. What is the song title?
2. And I can see you years from now in a bar, Talking over a football game, With that same big loud opinion, But nobody's listening. What song is it?
3. Which song did Taylor write about a redneck who's really bad at lying?
4. Taylor Swift has stated that ___ is her lucky number.
5. In the song "Fearless" where did she say she would dance with him?
6. Finish the lyrics from "A Place In This World": "Got the radio on, ___ And I'm wearing my heart on ___"
7. In which Taylor Swift video does this conversation occur? Boy: "All I want is you. Do you love me?" Taylor: "Yeah." Boy: "Can you give me another chance?" Taylor: "No."
8. What song are these lyrics from? "Standing by and waiting at your back door. All this time how could you not know."
9. Which two songs mention kissing in the rain?
10. What fits in the blank from "Tied Together With A Smile"? "You cry but you don't tell anyone that you might not be _____"

ANSWERS QUIZ 20

1. Dear John
2. Mean
3. Picture to Burn
4. 13
5. In a storm
6. My old blue jeans; my sleeve
7. White Horse
8. You Belong With Me
9. Hey Stephen and "The Way I Loved You"
10. The golden one

QUIZ 21

1. Not Scared?
2. I see your face in my mind as I drive away, cause none of us thought it was gonna end that way. What song is this lyric from?
3. In "Tim McGraw," what month is Taylor talking about when she's glad her boyfriend's gone?
4. Fill in the blank: "Music starts playing like _____"
5. In "Fearless", what type of a town is the singer in?
6. You said the way my blue eyes shine, starts off what song?
7. Fill in the missing word to these lyrics. "You have a way of coming _____ to me"?
8. Fill in the blank. "Drew looks at me, I _____ a smile so he won't see."
9. Which song was the second to be released as a video from Taylor Swift's self titled CD?
10. 'Baby and you might still have me' is taken from which song?

ANSWERS QUIZ 21

1. Fearless
2. Breathe
3. September
4. the end of a sad movie
5. One-horse
6. Tim McGraw
7. easily
8. fake
9. Teardrops On My Guitar
10. Should've Said No

QUIZ 22

1. Which sappy love song features these lyrics? "This ain't for the best/ my reputation's never been worse/ so you must like me for me"
2. This ain't for the best, my reputation's never been worse, so, you must like me for me. These are the opening lines to which song?
3. From "White Horse": "This ain't _____, this is a small town." Which of the following completes the lyric?
4. I remember when we broke up the first time Saying, This is it, I've had enough," 'cause like We hadn't seen each other in a month When you said you needed space." Which song are these lyrics taken from?
5. Evil Red Liquid What song is this, in other words?
6. The lyrics "Every night with us is like a dream" comes from which song?
7. You always knew how to push my buttons, you give me everything and nothing, this mad mad love makes you come running, to stand back where you stood. Which of the following is the correct song?
8. What time is mentioned in "Last Kiss"?
9. Finish the line; "Missing him was dark grey _____"
10. Does Taylor hide messages in the song lyrics for this album by capitalizing certain letters?

ANSWERS QUIZ 22

1. Delicate
2. Delicate
3. Hollywood
4. We Are Never Ever Getting Back Together
5. Bad Blood
6. New Romantics
7. I Wish You Would
8. 1:58am
9. All alone
10. Mostly

QUIZ 23

1. Get me with those green eyes, baby, as the lights go down. What song are these lyrics from?
2. Besides the song "Red", what other songs from the "Red" album have the word "red" in the lyrics?
3. Fill in the blank: "But sophistication isn't what you _____ or who you know..."
4. Say you're sorry, that face of an angel comes out just when you need it to... This first line is from which song from "Fearless"?
5. I'm really gonna miss you picking fights, and me falling for it screaming that I'm right, and you would hide away and find your peace of mind, with some indie record that's much cooler than mine. What song it this?
6. What song has this quote? "It's a ____ _____ baby just say yes."
7. What's this song? "Time slows down whenever you're around"
8. What song are these lyrics from? "The way you move is like a full-on rainstorm"
9. Who famously interrupted Taylor's acceptance speech at the 2009 MTV Video Music Awards for Best Female Video?
10. Which word is missing? "I don't know why, but with you, I'd dance in a storm in my . . ."

ANSWERS QUIZ 23

1. Sparks Fly
2. All Too Well and "The Moment I Knew"
3. wear
4. White Horse
5. We Are Never Ever Getting Back Together
6. Love Story
7. Today Was a Fairytale
8. Sparks Fly
9. Kanye West
10. best dress

QUIZ 24

1. What type of music does Taylor Swift sing?
2. From "Cold As You": "Oh what a shame, what a _____ ending given to a perfect day". Complete the lyric.
3. Many numbers are mentioned in the song "Mary's Song (Oh My My My)". Which of these ages is not in the song?
4. Which song has this line? "Come on, come on, don't leave me like this!"
5. Return to the Twelfth Month?
6. I miss your tan skin, your sweet smile, so good to me, so right. This is a line from which song?
7. What is the last line in 'Sparks Fly'?
8. 'State the obvious I didn't get my perfect fantasy'. Which lyric comes next?
9. The song "Dear John" was widely rumored to be about which of the following celebrities?
10. Which song has this line? "You could take me down with just one single blow".

ANSWERS QUIZ 24

1. Country music
2. rainy
3. twenty-six
4. Haunted
5. Back to December
6. Back to December
7. sparks fly
8. I realised you love yourself more then you could ever love me
9. John Mayer
10. Mean

QUIZ 25

1. Wasn't it beautiful when you believed in everything? And everybody believed in you? Which of these song is it?
2. Which song did Taylor write about a guy who she can't help but want to kiss in the rain?
3. What was the name of the guy whose name appeared as a hidden message in 'Should've Said No'?
4. What song did Colbie Caillat feature in?
5. Fill in the lyric to "Tim McGraw": "Just a boy in a ___ That had a tendency of getting stuck on backroads at night"
6. Where does the video for "Change" take place?
7. What song do these lyrics match up with? "Once upon a time I believe it was a Tuesday when I caught your eye, and we caught on to something. I hold on to the night. You looked me in the eyes and told me you loved me."
8. Which two songs mention putting up walls?
9. What fits in the blank, from "Mary's Song"? I'll be ___ and you'll be 89
10. Affection Tale?

ANSWERS QUIZ 25

1. Innocent
2. Hey Stephen
3. Sam
4. Breathe
5. Chevy Truck
6. a church
7. Forever and Always
8. Cold as You and "Change"
9. 87
10. Love Story

QUIZ 26

1. They might be bigger, but we're faster and never scared! What song is this lyric from?
2. What's the song with Taylor singing the melody and Colbie Caillat's harmony?
3. What song is this from? "Try to stay out of everybody's way."
4. In "Fifteen", what has the singer "found"?
5. Fill in the blank for the song "Fearless" "In this _____"
6. What was Taylor's first number one song that was on "Billboard Magazine" Hot Country Songs chart?
7. What is Taylor Swift's middle name?
8. What is the song when she compares someone to being "the song in the car I keep singing don't know why I do"?
9. Fill in the missing words to this lyric. "And my old faded..."
10. What color dress is Taylor wearing in her video for "Teardrops On My Guitar?"

ANSWERS QUIZ 26

1. Change
2. Breathe
3. Fifteen
4. Time can heal most anything
5. one-horse town
6. Our Song
7. Alison
8. Teardrops on My Guitar
9. blue jeans
10. Green

QUIZ 27

1. 'Nobody ever, lets me in' is part of which song?
2. Our secret moments/ in a crowded room/ they got no idea/ about me and you are the opening lines from which song?
3. All my flowers grew back as thorns, windows boarded up after the storm, he built a fire just to keep me warm. What song is it?
4. From "Ours": "And any snide remarks from my father about your _____ will be ignored." What word completes the lyric?
5. 'Cause you got that ____ daydream look in your eye And I got that red lip, classic thing that you like And when we go crashing down, we come back every time 'Cause we never go out of style, we never go out of style Which actor goes in the blanks to complete the above lyrics?
6. Empty Area What song is this, in other words?
7. I said 'I've been there too a few times'. Which song are these lyrics from?
8. Cause they got the cages, they got the boxes, and guns, they are the hunters, we are the foxes, and we run. Which song is this?
9. In what year did Taylor Swift win her first Grammy Award?
10. Finish the line; "32 and _____"

ANSWERS QUIZ 27

1. The Outside
2. Dress
3. Call It What You Want
4. tattoos
5. James Dean
6. Blank Space
7. Style
8. I Know Places
9. 2010
10. Still growing up now

QUIZ 28

1. What song is this from, and what comes next? "Tonight I'm gonna dance, for all that we've been through, but I don't wanna dance, I I'm not dancing with..."
2. I talked to your dad, go pick out a white dress. Which of these songs do these lyrics belong to?
3. What city is mentioned in both "Holy Ground" and "Come Back...Be Here"?
4. Fill in the blank: "I'm a _____ up piece of paper lying here..."
5. In the first line of "Mine", what is Taylor's boyfriend's job?
6. And I'll do anything you say, if you say it with your hands, and I'd be smart to walk away, but you're quicksand. Which of these songs are these from?
7. In what song does Taylor Swift say, "I can't help it if you look like an angel, and I can't help it if I want to kiss you in the rain..."?
8. Which is a song on her "Fearless" album?
9. What song does the beginning of this chorus belong to? "So this is me swallowing my pride"
10. Which Taylor Swift song is the odd one out in terms of the album it appeared on?

ANSWERS QUIZ 28

1. 'Holy Ground'- You
2. Love Story
3. New York City
4. crumpled
5. Part-time waiter
6. Treacherous
7. Hey Stephen
8. Fifteen
9. Back to December
10. Our Song

QUIZ 29

1. One song on Taylor Swift's "Fearless" CD has a title that's a number. What song is it?
2. Which of Taylor's songs do these lyrics come from "But in a box beneath my bed, is a letter that you never read"?
3. What song does this lyric belong to? "You had me falling for you honey, I never would've gone away"?
4. From "Forever and Always": "Did I say something way too _____, made you run and hide?" Finish this line.
5. What is the first name of Taylor Swift's brother?
6. At fourteen there's just so much you can't do, And you can't wait to move out someday and call your own shots. Which song are these lyrics from?
7. Identify this song: "Horrified looks from everyone in the room..."
8. Belongs to Me?
9. So baby drive slow 'Til we run out of road I'm trying so hard not to get caught up now. Which song is this?
10. What is the first line in 'Back to December'?

ANSWERS QUIZ 29

1. Fifteen
2. Tim McGraw
3. You're Not Sorry
4. honest
5. Austin
6. Never Grow Up
7. Speak Now
8. Mine
9. Fearless
10. I'm so glad you made time to see me

QUIZ 30

1. According to popular rumor, 'Forever and Always' was written about which singer?
2. It is widely believed that Taylor Swift writes hidden messages in her songs. According to Taylor, what is the hidden message in 'Fifteen'?
3. Taylor has a song on the album "Speak Now" called "Last Kiss". Finish the lyrics: "All that I know is I don't know how to be something you ___".
4. In a Christian wedding ceremony, a preacher will often say two words before allowing anyone to express his or her opinion against the marriage. Taylor wrote a song about this called ___. Please state the song name.
5. Your eyes whispered have we met?" Across the room your silhouette, Starts to make its way to me." What song is it?
6. Which song's music video won a VMA?
7. What was the first song Taylor ever wrote?
8. In the song "Stay Beautiful", whose eyes are like a jungle?
9. Which line from "You Belong With Me" is contradicted in its video?
10. What song do these lyrics go to? "These walls that they put up to hold us back will fall down. It's a revolution the time will come for us to finally win."

ANSWERS QUIZ 30

1. Joe Jonas
2. I cried while recording this
3. miss
4. Speak Now
5. Enchanted
6. You Belong With Me
7. Lucky You
8. Corey's
9. I remember you driving to my house
10. Change

QUIZ 31

1. Which of these songs does NOT mention a father or a daddy in the lyrics?
2. What fits in the blank from the song, "You Belong With Me"? "She wears high heels, I wear _____"
3. Inhale Air?
4. I'm sick and tired of your attitude. I'm feeling like I don't know you. What song is this lyric from?
5. Finish the lyric: "...I won't pick up the phone. This is the ____ _____, don't wanna hurt anymore..."
6. What song is this from? "You're just so cool, run your hands through your hair"
7. In "Love Story", where was the singer crying and "begging you please don't go"?
8. What song was about Taylor and her friend Abigail?
9. Finish the lyrics: "She said, I was _____"
10. What is Taylor's hometown and state?

ANSWERS QUIZ 31

1. A Place in This World
2. sneakers
3. Breathe
4. Tell Me Why
5. last straw
6. Fearless
7. The staircase
8. Fifteen
9. 7 and you were 9
10. Wyomissing, Pennsylvania

QUIZ 32

1. What song has the lyrics, "I almost didn't notice all the roses and a note that said..."?
2. Select the missing word. "I can't even see _____ when he's with me"
3. Fill in the blanks. "He says he's so in love, he's finally got it _____ I wonder if he knows he's all I think about at _____."
4. What color is the dress mentioned in the song "Tim McGraw"?
5. Which song mentions 'Drew'?
6. Name the song featuring these lyrics: "See you in the dark/ all eyes on you/ my magician/ all eyes on us"
7. Big reputation, big reputation, oh, you and me would be a big conversation. What song is this?
8. From "State of Grace": "Love is a _____ game, unless you play it good and right." Which of the following completes the lyric?
9. So this is me swallowing my pride, Standing in front of you saying I'm sorry for that night. Which song contains these lyrics?
10. Sacred Land What song is this, in other words?

ANSWERS QUIZ 32

1. Our Song
2. anyone
3. right, night
4. Black
5. Teardrops on My Guitar
6. So It Goes...
7. End Game
8. ruthless
9. Back to December
10. Holy Ground

QUIZ 33

1. Which popular song from her album contains the lyrics "Cause darling I'm a nightmare, dressed like a daydream"?
2. I want you for worse or for better, I would wait forever and ever, broke your heart, I'll put it back together. What song do these lyrics belong to?
3. What is the first age mentioned in 'The Best Day'?
4. Finish this line; "Take a deep breath and _____"
5. Which song was the first to be released as a single from this album in the UK?
6. Besides red, what other colors are mentioned in the chorus of "Red"?
7. What article of clothing is in the lyrics of "Dear John", "Better Than Revenge", "Holy Ground", and "The Moment I Knew"?
8. Fill in the blank: "The _____ question kept me up..."
9. Put your lips close to mine, as long as they don't touch... this first line comes from which song?
10. You find yourself at my door, just like all those times before, you wear your best apology, but I was there to watch you leave. What song are these from?

ANSWERS QUIZ 33

1. Blank Space
2. How You Get The Girl
3. Five
4. Walk through the door
5. We Are Never Ever Getting Back Together
6. blue and gray
7. dress
8. lingering
9. Treacherous
10. The Last Time

QUIZ 34

1. Which song is on her "Speak Now" album?
2. What song are these lyrics from? "I am not the kind of girl who should be rudely barging in on a white veil occasion."
3. In which film did Taylor Swift NOT appear?
4. Which word completes this sentence? This is from "Change". "Throw your hands up, 'cause we never gave. . ."
5. What instrument does Taylor Swift play?
6. What song does this lyric belong to? "You sit in class next to a red-headed Abigail and soon enough you're best friends"?
7. From "Never Grow Up": "You're in the car on the way to the _____". What word goes in the blank?
8. What was the first single released by Taylor?
9. Which of Taylor's songs from her first three albums has a number for a title?
10. Which song has this line? "And grumbling on about how I can't sing..."

ANSWERS QUIZ 34

1. The Story Of Us
2. Speak Now
3. The Last Song
4. in
5. Guitar
6. Fifteen
7. movies
8. Tim McGraw
9. Fifteen
10. Mean

QUIZ 35

1. Talk Right This Instant?
2. And I lived in your chess games, but you changed the rules everyday. Which song has this line?
3. What kind of a city will Taylor be living in, in 'Mean'?
4. When was Taylor Swift born?
5. In the song 'I'd Lie', whose eyes does the boy have?
6. Another song on Taylor's album "Speak Now" is "Mean". Finish the lyrics: "Someday I'll be living in a big ole ___".
7. In one song, what does Taylor want her child to do?
8. Don't you think I was too young, To be messed with, The girl in the dress,  Cried the whole way home, I should've known. Which song is it?
9. Which song was inspired by Taylor's eventful freshman year at Hendersonville High School?
10. Who is Austin Swift?

ANSWERS QUIZ 35

1. speak now
2. Dear John
3. Big old city
4. 13-Dec-89
5. his father's
6. city
7. Never Grow Up
8. Dear John
9. Fifteen
10. Taylor's brother

QUIZ 36

1. In the song "Forever and Always", what day was it when she caught his eye?
2. Finish the lyric to "Our Song": "I was walking up the front porch steps After everything that day had gone all wrong Or been trampled on and lost and thrown away. Got into the hallway, well on my way to my ___, I almost didn't notice all the roses And the note that said..."
3. What does Taylor fantasize about doing in "Picture To Burn"?
4. What song do these lyrics go to? "I don't know why all the trees change in the fall. I know your not scared of anything at all. I don't know if snow whites house is near or far away."
5. Which two songs have lyrics that talk about marriage proposals?
6. What fits in the blank from "Love Story"? "My faith in you was fading, when I met you on the _____"
7. Unseen?
8. Why are people always leaving? I think you and I should stay the same. What song is this lyric from?
9. Finish-the-lyric: "Cory's eyes are like a _____"
10. Baby, what happened, please tell me 'cause one second it was _____, now you're halfway out the door.

ANSWERS QUIZ 36

1. Tuesday
2. lovin' bed
3. vandalizing the boy's house
4. The Best Day
5. Love Story and "Mary's Song (Oh My My My)"
6. Outskirts of town
7. Invisible
8. Hey Stephen
9. jungle
10. perfect

QUIZ 37

1. In "Hey Stephen", the singer thought she'd never see someone _____ the way he does.
2. In the song "Love Story" complete this lyric: "This love is difficult but it's..."
3. What was Taylor's first U.S. single?
4. How old was Taylor when she joined Big Machine Records?
5. What song talks about "our mamas smiled and rolled their eyes"?
6. Select one of the following words to make this lyric true. "Don't know what's down this road I'm just..."
7. Fill in the blank. "Drew walks by me, can he tell that I can't _____?"
8. In "Our Song", when she got home before she said amen, what does she ask God to do?
9. 'Hoping it will end up in his pocket' is taken from which song?
10. There's glitter on the floor/ after the party/ girls carrying their shoes/ down in the lobby What song are these lyrics from?

ANSWERS QUIZ 37

1. Shine
2. real
3. Tim McGraw
4. 15
5. Mary's Song (Oh my, my, my)
6. walking
7. breathe
8. play it again
9. Tied Together With a Smile
10. New Year's Day

QUIZ 38

1. Met you in a bar, all eyes on me, your illusionist, all eyes on us. Which of the following are these lyrics from?
2. From "I Know Places": "They are the hunters, we are the _____." What word goes in the blank?
3. I guess you didn't care And I guess I liked that And when I fell hard You took a step back Without me, without me, without me Name the song which contains these lyrics.
4. Hygienic What song is this, in other words?
5. Been losing grip, oh, sinking ships You showed up just in time is from what song?
6. When we first dropped our bags on apartment floors, took our broken hearts, put them in a drawer, everybody here was someone else before. What song is it?
7. 'It's 2am I'm cursing your name' is from what song?
8. Finish this line; "This slope is_____"
9. Which song has the lyrics... "In my dreams you're touching my face, and asking me if I want to try again with you"?
10. From "State of Grace": "Up in your room and our slates are clean, just twin fire signs, four ___ eyes." What goes in the blank?

ANSWERS QUIZ 38

1. So It Goes...
2. foxes
3. I Knew You Were Trouble
4. Clean
5. This Love
6. Welcome To New York
7. The Way I loved You
8. Treacherous
9. I Almost Do
10. blue

QUIZ 39

1. What sport is included in the lyrics of "Mean" and "Stay Stay Stay"?
2. Fill in the blank: "I'm not a _____; this ain't a fairy tale."
3. Which car is mentioned in the first line of "Red"?
4. I'm walking fast through the traffic lights, busy streets and busy lives, and all we know is touch and go. What song it this?
5. Once upon a time, I believe it was a _____ when I caught your eye. What day is that?
6. Which song is on her "Taylor Swift" album?
7. What song are these lyrics from? "Long were the nights when my days once revolved around you"
8. Which one of these songs featured another singer with Taylor Swift?
9. We were both young when I first saw you. I close my eyes and the flashback starts. . . What song is this from?
10. Taylor Swift's song, "Back to December" is about whom?

ANSWERS QUIZ 39

1. football
2. princess
3. Maserati
4. State of Grace
5. Tuesday
6. Picture to Burn
7. Dear John
8. Breathe
9. Love Story
10. Taylor Lautner

QUIZ 40

1. What song does this lyric belong to? "so we've been outnumbered, raided and now cornered"
2. From "Tied Together With a Smile": "Seems the only one who doesn't see your beauty is the _____ in the mirror looking back at you." What is the missing word?
3. In 2008, Taylor Swift was publicly dating Joe Jonas from the pop/rock band The Jonas Brothers. After their break-up, what song was rumored to be about him from the album "Fearless"?
4. What time is mentioned in "Mine"?
5. Name the song that this lyric belongs to: "Never imagined we'd end like this Your name, forever the name on my lips"
6. Don't Become Older?
7. And it's not theirs to speculate if it's wrong And your hands are tough but they are where mine belong. Identify the song.
8. 'Seems like there's always someone who ___'. What word fills in the blank from the song 'Ours'?
9. In an interview, Taylor stated that she had a lucky number. What was it?
10. In 'Mine', what time was the fight?

ANSWERS QUIZ 40

1. Change
2. face
3. Forever and Always
4. 2:30 a.m.
5. Last Kiss
6. Never Grow Up
7. Ours
8. disapproves
9. 13
10. 2:30 AM

QUIZ 41

1. Taylor's CD "Speak Now" hit stores in the US on which date?
2. Which song has this line in it: "I'm a house of cards"?
3. Drop everything now, Meet me in the pouring rain, Kiss me on the sidewalk, Take away the pain. Which of the following songs is it?
4. In which song is the guy not going to be able to catch her?
5. Which one of these songs was dedicated to Taylor's mother?
6. In the song "Love Story", where did "Romeo" propose?
7. In the third verse of "Teardrops On My Guitar", why does she laugh?
8. Which of these is NOT one of the scenes from "Our Song"?
9. What song are these lyrics from? "You could write a book on how to ruin some one's perfect day. Well I get so confused and frustrated. Forget what I'm trying to say, oh."
10. Which day of the week is mentioned in both "Forever and Always" and "You Belong With Me"?

ANSWERS QUIZ 41

1. 25-Oct-10
2. Sparks Fly
3. Sparks Fly
4. White Horse
5. The Best Day
6. on the outskirts of town
7. 'cause it's so damn funny
8. Taylor driving in a car
9. Tell Me Why
10. Tuesday

QUIZ 42

1. What fits in the blank from "Picture to Burn"? "So go and tell your friends that I'm _____ and crazy that's fine"
2. Continue to be Pretty?
3. Well, count to ten, take it in. This is life before you know who you're gonna be. What song is this lyric from?
4. Which song alludes to Romeo and Juliet?
5. What song is this from? "Makes me run for cover when you're around"
6. In "White Horse", what does the singer say she always wanted him to do?
7. How many reasons did Taylor say she could give Stephen for choosing her in the song "Hey Stephen"?
8. How many reasons did Taylor say she could give Stephen for choosing her in the song "Hey Stephen"?
9. What was Taylor's second U.S. single?
10. How old was Taylor when her first single was released?

ANSWERS QUIZ 42

1. obsessive
2. Stay Beautiful
3. Fifteen
4. Love Story
5. Tell Me Why
6. Beg for her
7. 50
8. 50
9. Teardrops on my Guitar
10. 16

QUIZ 43

1. Which song talks about someone having eyes "like a jungle and a smile like a radio"?
2. Fill in the missing word. "I didn't know what I would find when I went looking for a..."
3. Fill in the blank. "There he goes so _____"
4. Finish this lyric from "A Place In This World."-- "Tomorrow's just a mystery Oh yeah... "
5. Which song was the first hit on this CD?
6. Knew he was a killer/ first time that I saw him/ wondering how many girls/ he had loved and left haunted The opening lyrics from which song on "Reputation"?
7. I could've spent forever with your hands in my pockets, picture of your face in an invisible locket, you said there was nothing in the world that could stop it, I had a bad feeling. Which song is it?
8. From "Safe & Sound": "Hold onto this _____ even when the music's gone." What word completes this line?
9. Dear ___, I see it all now that you're gone Don't you think I was too young to be messed with? The girl in the dress, cried the whole way home, I should've known Which name goes in the blanks to complete these lyrics?
10. Start Once More What song is this, in other words?

ANSWERS QUIZ 43

1. Stay Beautiful
2. reason
3. perfectly
4. but that's okay
5. Tim McGraw
6. ...Ready For It?
7. Dancing With Our Hands Tied
8. lullaby
9. John
10. Begin Again

QUIZ 44

1. Which song do the lyrics "And life was never worse, but never better" come from?
2. Band-aids don't fix bullet holes, you say sorry just for show, you live like that, you live with ghosts. Which song are these lyrics from?
3. On which social media app did Taylor have ten million plus followers by 2014?
4. It feels like a perfect night to dress up like_____ Finish the line.
5. What comes next? 'Cause all I know is we said hello, your eyes looked like...'
6. Fill in the blank in this song title: "___ Horse".
7. Which of these songs does NOT mention cars?
8. Fill in the blank: "_____ don't leave me like this"
9. In the first line of "Mean", what simile is used to describe the critic's words?
10. And he's long gone when he's next to me, and I realize the blame is on me. What song are these lyrics from?

ANSWERS QUIZ 44

1. Wonderland
2. Bad Blood
3. Instagram
4. Hipsters
5. Coming home
6. white
7. Last Kiss
8. Come on, come on
9. Like knives and swords and weapons that you use against me
10. I Knew You Were Trouble

QUIZ 45

1. What song are these lyrics from? "Do you remember we were sitting there by the water"
2. What comes after these lyrics in "Mean"? "You with your words"
3. Which of these is NOT a Taylor Swift song?
4. She wears short skirts, I wear T-shirts. What song is this from?
5. What was the first song that Taylor Swift wrote?
6. What song does this lyric belong to? "All those other girls, well, they're beautiful, but would they write a song for you"?
7. From "Hey Stephen": "All those other girls, well they're _____, but would they write a song for you?" Fill in the blank.
8. In which movie did Taylor Swift play the role of Felicia?
9. From "Dear John": "Dear John, I see it all now it was wrong, Don't you think ___'s too young, To be played by your dark, twisted games." What number goes in the blank?
10. Choose the song with these words: "Flash forward and we're taking on the world together".

ANSWERS QUIZ 45

1. Mine
2. like knives
3. Who Says
4. You Belong With Me
5. Lucky You
6. Hey Stephen
7. beautiful
8. Valentine's Day
9. nineteen
10. Mine

QUIZ 46

1. Not Guilty?
2. Every smile you fake is so condescending, counting all the scars you made   Which song has this verse?
3. 'The stakes are high, the water's __'. What word completes this line?
4. Taylor Swift mentions her brother in the song 'Best Day'. What is his name? Note: His name is not said in the song.
5. In 'Sparks Fly', when does Taylor say she sees sparks fly?
6. Taylor had bonus songs on her album's deluxe US edition. Which of these was one of the bonus tracks?
7. In the song "Back to December", it was rumored that Taylor was singing about a previous boyfriend who starred in the "Twilight" movies. Name him.
8. I said remember this moment, in the back of my mind, The time we stood with our shaking hands, The crowds in stands went wild. Which of these songs is it?
9. What song is based on a guy called Cory?
10. Which character did Taylor portray in the film 'Valentine's Day'?

ANSWERS QUIZ 46

1. Innocent
2. Cold As You
3. rough
4. Austin
5. whenever you smile
6. Ours
7. Taylor Lautner
8. Long Live
9. Stay Beautiful
10. Felicia

QUIZ 47

1. In the song "The Best Day", she found a video from when she was what age?
2. At the start of "Mary's Song (Oh My My My)", the lyrics state: "She said, I was seven and you were nine". How old does she say they are at the end of the song?
3. What color dress is Taylor Swift wearing in her room in the "Teardrops on My Guitar" video?
4. What is the name of the song these lyrics are from? "So baby drive slow, 'Til we run out of road in this one horse town I want to stay right here, in the passenger seat you put your eyes on me, live this moment now capture it remember it."
5. Hey Stephen: "'Cause I can't help it if you look like a(n) _____" "White Horse": "That face of a(n) _____ comes out just when you need it to" What word should go in both blanks?
6. What fits in the blank from "I'm only me when I'm with you"? "'Cause I'm only up when _____"
7. Photo To Incinerate?
8. I don't know why all the trees change in the fall, but I know that you're not scared of anything at all. What song is this lyric from?
9. In "White Horse," what might the heroine have been, lost in his eyes?
10. What goes in the blank? "Don't know if _____ house is near or far away."

ANSWERS QUIZ 47

1. 3
2. 87 and 89
3. green
4. Fearless
5. angel
6. You're not down
7. Picture to Burn
8. The Best Day
9. naive
10. Snow White's

QUIZ 48

1. In "You Belong with Me", what "typical" night is it?
2. Which song contains this lyric: "my mistake I didn't know to be in love you had to fight to have the upper hand"?
3. Where is Taylor originally from?
4. How old was Taylor when she began writing songs and playing the guitar?
5. What song talks about giving love away "like it's extra change" ?
6. Which word is the correct answer? "Seems the only one who doesn't see your..."
7. Fill in the blank. "The kind of _____ I wish I could be."
8. Finish this lyric from "Mary's Song (Oh My My My)". "When I'll be 87 you'll be __"
9. 'State the obvious' is the first line to which song?
10. It was so nice/ having big parties/ jumping in the pool/ from the balcony Name this song?

ANSWERS QUIZ 48

1. Tuesday
2. White Horse
3. Wyomissing, Pennsylvania
4. 12
5. Tied Together With a Smile
6. beauty
7. flawless
8. 89
9. Picture to Burn
10. This Is Why We Can't Have Nice Things

QUIZ 49

1. Knew I was a robber, first time that he saw me, stealing hearts and running off and never saying sorry. Which Taylor Swift song is this?
2. From "Mean": "You, with your words like knives and _____ and weapons that you use against me." What word fills in the blank?
3. Not In The Forest What song is this, in other words?
4. You two are dancing in a snow globe, round and round is from which song?
5. I never miss a beat, I'm lightning on my feet, and that's what they don't see. Which of the following is the correct song?
6. How old was Taylor when she wrote her first song, 'Lucky You'?
7. What are the missing words? "I was there I _____ all too well"
8. Name the bonus track.
9. What holiday is mentioned in "Begin Again" and "The Moment I Knew"?
10. Fill in the blank. "So I sneak out to the _____ to see you."

ANSWERS QUIZ 49

1. ...Ready For It?
2. swords
3. Out Of The Woods
4. You Are In Love
5. Shake It Off
6. 12
7. Remember it
8. Girl at Home
9. Christmas
10. garden

QUIZ 50

1. How old is Taylor in the first line of "The Best Day"?
2. Now it's big black cars and Riviera views, and your lover in the foyer doesn't even know you, and your secrets end up splashed on the news front page. What song is it?
3. What Taylor Swift song is this? "It turns out freedom ain't nothin' but missin' you wishin' I realized what I had when you were mine."
4. What song does this belong to? "Can't you see that I'm the one that understands you"
5. What is this song? "And I don't know how it gets better than this you take my hand and drag me headfirst"
6. Taylor plays all of the following instruments EXCEPT:
7. Which of these is not a song on this album?
8. Does Taylor Swift have any siblings?
9. What goes in the blank of the Taylor Swift quote? "This is definitely the highlight of my _____ year"?
10. From "Better Than Revenge": "She had to know the _____ was beating in me like a drum". Which of these words fill in the blank?

ANSWERS QUIZ 50

1. Five
2. The Lucky One
3. Back to December
4. You Belong With Me
5. Fearless
6. Flute
7. Sparks Fly
8. Yes, a brother named Austin
9. Senior
10. pain

QUIZ 51

1. In 2009, Taylor Swift publicly dated which "Twilight" actor?
2. From "The Way I Loved You": "But I miss screaming and fighting and kissing in the rain, And it's ___ a.m. and I'm cursing your name." What number fills in the blank?
3. What song has this verse? "And the story of us Looks a lot like a tragedy now Next chapter"
4. Not Nice?
5. I know people change and these things happen But I remember how it was back then Locked up in your arms and our friends are laughing 'Cause nothing like this ever happened to them. This line is from which song?
6. 'Lost your balance on a ____'. What's the missing word? This line is from the song 'Innocent'.
7. What is Taylor's middle name?
8. In 'Mary's Song (Oh My My My)', where does the boy propose?
9. Taylor named one of her songs after which superhero?
10. Flash forward and we're taking on the world together, And there's a drawer of my things at your place. What song is it?

ANSWERS QUIZ 51

1. Taylor Lautner
2. two
3. The Story of Us
4. Mean
5. If This Was a Movie
6. tightrope
7. Alison
8. at their favourite spot in town
9. Superman
10. Mine

QUIZ 52

1. Which song did Taylor write when she was just 12?
2. Which musician was rumored to have inspired the song 'Forever and Always'?
3. What song is a girl tired of being last to know?
4. In the song "Should've Said No", how many times is the chorus sung?
5. In the "Love Story" video, who plays Romeo?
6. What song is this? "That you were Romeo you were throwing pebbles, And my daddy said stay away from Juliet, And I was crying on the staircase begging you, Please don't go."
7. What time is mentioned in both "Breathe" and "The Way I Loved You"?
8. What fits in the blank from "Our Song"? "Took out a pen and _____ and I, wrote down our song"
9. Ivory Equine?
10. I keep waiting for you but you never come. What song is this lyric from?

ANSWERS QUIZ 52

1. A Place In This World
2. Joe Jonas
3. You're Not Sorry
4. 3
5. Justin Gaston
6. Love Story
7. two a.m.
8. an old napkin
9. White Horse
10. Love Story

QUIZ 53

1. In a song, a girl falls in love with a childhood friend and lives her whole life with him. Name the girl? (hint: the song name)
2. Fill in the blank to this second verse: "'Cause you were Romeo, _____."
3. Which song contains the lyric: "And you've got a smile that could light up this whole town"?
4. Finish the lyrics.... "I hate that stupid old _____"
5. Which song talks about "striking a match on all my wasted time"?
6. Fill in the missing word to make this lyric true. "There's pretty girls on every..."
7. Fill in the blank. "He's the _____ in the car, I keep singing don't know why I do."
8. Which songs starts off "I didn't know what I would find"?
9. 'Oh, what a shame' starts off the chorus to which song?
10. I'm perfectly fine/ I live on my own/ I've made up my mind/ I'm better off being alone What song is this?

ANSWERS QUIZ 53

1. Mary
2. I was a scarlet letter
3. You Belong With Me
4. pick up truck, you never let me drive
5. Picture to Burn
6. corner
7. song
8. The Outside
9. Cold as You
10. King of My Heart

QUIZ 54

1. Please don't ever become a stranger, whose laugh I could recognize anywhere. What song is this?
2. From "Everything Has Changed": "And all I've seen since eighteen hours ago is green eyes and ____ and your smile." Which of the following goes in the blank?
3. You can plan for a change in weather and time But I never planned on you changing your mind Which song are the above lines taken from?
4. Most Untamed Night Visions What song is this, in other words?
5. And to the fella over there, with the hella good hair comes from what upbeat 1989 song?
6. The drought was the very worst, when the flowers that we'd grown together died of thirst. These are the first lines of what song?
7. Taylor has stated in an interview that ___ is her lucky number. What is that number?
8. Finish the line; "I am not the kind of girl who should be rudely barging in on a____ occasion."
9. Which of these songs is sung by two singers?
10. The water's high, you're jumping into it, and letting go, and no one knows, that you cry, but you don't tell anyone, that you might not be the golden one. What song are these lyrics from?

ANSWERS QUIZ 54

1. New Year's Day
2. freckles
3. Last Kiss
4. Wildest Dreams
5. Shake It Off
6. Clean
7. 13
8. White veil
9. The Last Time
10. Tied Together With a Smile

QUIZ 55

1. Which two songs have boys with green eyes?
2. Fill in the blank. "In the heat of the fight I _____ away."
3. I was ridin' shotgun with my hair undone, in the front seat of his car... What song is this first line from?
4. Loving him is like driving a new Maserati down a dead-end street, faster than the wind, passionate as sin ending so suddenly. Which of these songs is it?
5. What two songs on her "Speak Now" album did Taylor write about John Mayer?
6. What is this song? "So this is me swallowing my pride standing in front of you saying I'm sorry for that night"
7. What song's chorus starts off like this? "'Cause when you're _____ and somebody tells you they love you, you're gonna believe them."
8. Choose the album that was not released by Taylor Swift.
9. Find the missing words. "I see your face in my mind as I. . ."
10. Which word/s is missing from these "Forever and Always" lyrics, "And I stare at the phone and he still hasn't called, and then you feel so low, you can't feel nothin' at all, and you _____ to when he said forever and always"

ANSWERS QUIZ 55

1. Sparks Fly and "Everything Has Changed"
2. walked
3. Our Song
4. Red
5. The Story of Us, and Dear John
6. Back to December
7. Fifteen
8. My World 2.0
9. drive away
10. Flashback

QUIZ 56

1. What song does this lyric belong to? "I'm five years old"?
2. From "Stay Beautiful": "If what you are is a _____ I'll never get to hold, I hope you know..." Which of these words goes in the blank?
3. Who was the director for Taylor's music video "Tim McGraw"?
4. It's okay, life is a tough crowd Thirty-two, and still growin' up now Who you are is not what you did. What song are these lyrics from?
5. Name the song that has this lyric: "Wondering which version of you I might get on the phone tonight".
6. Flares Become Airborne?
7. I wake up, I'm alive In only a little while, I cry 'Cause you're my lullaby So baby come hold me tight. Name this song.
8. Complete this line: 'Your little hand wrapped around my ___'.
9. The first song that Taylor wrote was 'Lucky You'. How old was she when she wrote it?
10. Finish this lyric: 'Walls of insincerity, shifting eyes and vacancy, ___'.

ANSWERS QUIZ 56

1. The Best Day
2. daydream
3. Trey Fanjoy
4. Innocent
5. Dear John
6. Sparks Fly
7. Beautiful Eyes
8. finger
9. 12
10. vanished when I saw your face

QUIZ 57

1. In the music video for "Mine", how many kids does Taylor have?
2. Which song was apparently written about an incident with Kanye West at the 2009 Video Music Awards?
3. I'd go back in time and change it but I can't, So if the chain is on your door I understand. Which song is it?
4. Which song featured Colbie Caillat?
5. What was Taylor's third album called?
6. In the song "The Way I Loved You" what time is it when she's cursing his name?
7. In the song "Tied Together with a Smile", how many times is the phrase "tied together with a smile" said?
8. Where is Taylor Swift for most of the "Tim McGraw" video? (Not including flashbacks).
9. What song is this? "If you and I are a story, That's never gets told, If what you are is a daydream I'll never get to hold, at least you'll know."
10. Cold as You: "Oh what a shame, what a rainy ending given to a _____ _____". "Tell Me Why": "You could write a book on how to ruin someone's _____ _____". What two words go in the blanks?

ANSWERS QUIZ 57

1. 2
2. Innocent
3. Back to December
4. Breathe
5. Speak Now
6. 2am
7. four
8. on a lakeshore
9. Stay Beautiful
10. perfect day

QUIZ 58

1. What fits in the blank from the song "Should've said no"? "Do you honestly expect me _____"
2. Alteration?
3. She wears high heels, I wear sneakers. She's cheer captain and I'm on the bleachers. What song is this lyric from?
4. What age is Taylor when she meets Abigail? (hint: song name)
5. What song is this from? "Can't help it if I want to kiss you in the rain."
6. In "Tell Me Why", what does the singer say he can write a book on?
7. Finish the lyric from the song "Breathe": "You're the only thing I know like..."?
8. Finish the lyric... "Just a ____" This is from the song "I'm Only Me When I'm With You" not "Tim McGraw".
9. One of Taylor's inspirations was a singer in her own family. Who inspired Taylor?
10. Which song talks about "wearing my heart on my sleeve"?

ANSWERS QUIZ 58

1. to believe
2. Change
3. You Belong With Me
4. fifteen
5. Hey Stephen
6. How to ruin someone's perfect day
7. the back of my hand
8. small town boy and girl
9. Her grandmother
10. A Place in this World

QUIZ 59

1. Fill in the missing word(s). "Do you honestly expect me to..."
2. Fill in the blank. "He's the _____ taken up, but there's never enough."
3. In "Tied Together With A Smile", even though the person is 'tied together with a smile,' what is still happening?
4. 'Sneakin' out late, tapping on your window' is part of which song's chorus?
5. My castle crumbled overnight/ I brought a knife to a gun fight/ they took the crown/ but it's alright What song is this?
6. I never trust a playboy, but they love me, so I fly 'em all around the world, and I let them think they saved me. Which of the following is correct?
7. From "Today Was a Fairytale": "You were the prince, I used to be a _____ in distress." Which word completes the line?
8. And I stare at the phone, he still hasn't called And then you feel so low you can't feel nothing at all And you flashback to when he said ___ Which song title completes the above lyrics?
9. Eleven Plus Eleven What song is this, in other words?
10. And the butterflies turned to dust they covered my whole room are lyrics from the song...

ANSWERS QUIZ 59

1. believe
2. time
3. The person's coming undone
4. Our Song
5. Call It What You Want
6. I Did Something Bad
7. damsel
8. Forever and Always
9. 22
10. Clean

QUIZ 60

1. So it's gonna be forever, or it's gonna go down in flames, you can tell me when it's over, if the high was worth the pain. These lyrics belong to what single?
2. How old was Taylor when she moved to Nashville?
3. Finish the line; "Love is a _____ game."
4. One of these is a correct Taylor Swift song title. Which one?
5. From "Everything Has Changed": "And all I've seen since eighteen hours ago, is ___ eyes and freckles and your smile." and "And all my walls stood tall painted ___." What words go in the blanks?
6. Which songs have the word "father" in their lyrics?
7. Fill in the blank. "____ should have been there."
8. I took a ... Complete the first line of "Tell Me Why".
9. All I knew this morning when I woke, is I know something now, know something now I didn't before. Which song are these lyrics from?
10. What comes next in the song "Stay, Stay, Stay" "I've been loving you for quite some time, time, time, you think that it's funny when I'm mad, mad, mad, but I think that it's best if __ ____ ____."

ANSWERS QUIZ 60

1. Blank Space
2. 14
3. Ruthless
4. Sad Beautiful Tragic
5. green, blue
6. Last Kiss, "Ours", and "Superman"
7. You
8. Chance
9. Everything Has Changed
10. We both stay

QUIZ 61

1. Drop everything now, meet me in the pouring rain, kiss me on the sidewalk, take away the pain What song is this?
2. What is this the chorus of? "Romeo save me I've been feeling so alone"
3. Which song was a deluxe edition track?
4. You don't have to call anymore, I won't pick up the phone. What song is this from?
5. What year did Taylor Swift win her first award?
6. What song does this lyric belong to? "That you were Romeo, I was a scarlet letter"?
7. From "Fifteen": "You sit in class next to a ____ named Abigail." What word goes in the blank?
8. From "Hey Stephen": "Hey Stephen, I could give you ___ reasons why I should be the one you choose." How many reasons can she give?
9. Pick the song with this line: "Drop everything now, meet me in the pouring rain".
10. The Tale of You and Me?

ANSWERS QUIZ 61

1. Sparks Fly
2. Love Story
3. Ours
4. You're Not Sorry
5. 2007
6. Love Story
7. redhead
8. fifty
9. Sparks Fly
10. The story of us

QUIZ 62

1. So I watch your life in pictures Like I used to watch you sleep And I feel you forget me Like I used to feel you breathe. Which song is this?
2. What board game is mentioned in the song 'Dear John'?
3. Which of these actors was Taylor Swift publicly dating in 2009?
4. According to the song 'Cold As You', where has Taylor never been?
5. The song "Innocent" was inspired by an incident with Kanye West, in which he had interrupted her 2009 VMA award acceptance speech. Kanye implied onstage that Taylor didn't deserve the award. Instead, which celebrity did he think had "one of the best videos of all time"?
6. In the song "Last Kiss", what time was it that Taylor "remembered the look on your face, lit through the darkness"?
7. I am not the kind of girl, Who should be rudely barging in on a white veil occasion. What song is it?
8. Which song did Taylor sing in a movie while playing a cameo?
9. How long did it take Taylor to write 'Love Story'?
10. In the song "White Horse", the face of something comes out when he needs it to. What is it?

ANSWERS QUIZ 62

1. Last Kiss
2. Chess
3. Taylor Lautner
4. anywhere as cold as you
5. Beyonce'
6. 1:58
7. Speak Now
8. Crazier
9. 20 minutes
10. Angel

QUIZ 63

1. In the song "Picture to Burn", what does she say she hates?
2. For a song from her "Fearless" CD, Taylor Swift plays two people in its music video. Which video?
3. What is this song? "I was riding shotgun with my hair undone in the front seat of his car, He has a one-hand feel on the steering wheel, The other on my heart."
4. Which article of clothing is in the lyrics of "Tim McGraw", "Love Story", and "Fearless"?
5. What fits in the blank from "Teardrops on My Guitar"? "_____ looks at me, I fake a smile so he won't see"
6. The Most Excellent Twenty-Four Hours?
7. I'm not the one you'll sweep off her feet, lead her up the stairwell. What song is this lyric from?
8. What song talks about Taylor Swift's mom?
9. What song is this from? "It's a roller coaster kinda rush."
10. Fill in the Blank: In "You're Not Sorry", he has his "share of _____."

ANSWERS QUIZ 63

1. His stupid old pickup truck
2. You Belong With Me
3. Our Song
4. Dress
5. Drew
6. The Best Day
7. White Horse
8. The Best Day
9. The Way I Loved You
10. secrets

QUIZ 64

1. Which song has the lyric: "You could write a book on how to ruin someone's perfect day"?
2. Finish the lyric... "I'm alone _____
3. How tall is Taylor Swift?
4. What song talks about "What a rainy ending given to a perfect day"?
5. Select the missing word. "A few _____ had gone and come around"
6. Fill in the blank again! "And he's all I need to _____ into."
7. In "Picture To Burn", what is it about the pickup truck that she doesn't like?
8. 'I don't know what I want, so don't ask me' starts off which of these songs?
9. I never trust a narcissist/ but they love me/ so I play 'em like a violin/ and I make it look oh so easy These are the first lines from what song?
10. And therein lies the issue, friends don't try to trick you, get you on the phone and mind-twist you. What song is it?

ANSWERS QUIZ 64

1. Tell Me Why
2. on my own
3. 5'11"
4. Cold As You
5. years
6. fall
7. he never lets her drive it
8. A Place in This World
9. I Did Something Bad
10. This Is Why We Can't Have Nice Things

QUIZ 65

1. From "Ronan": "We're gonna fly away from here, out of this curtained room in this _____ grey, we'll just disappear." What word fills in this blank?
2. You say that you'd take it all back, given one chance It was a moment of weakness and you said yes Name the song these lines are taken from.
3. The Final Instant What song is this, in other words?
4. Can you guess which song the lyrics "Then, why'd you have to go and lock me out when I let you in" comes from?
5. We're so young but we're on the road to ruin, we play dumb but we know exactly what we're doing, we cry tears of mascara in the bathroom, honey, life is just a classroom. What Deluxe Edition song is this?
6. When is Taylor's birthday?
7. Finish the line; "And he just might make me _____"
8. Which song from "Red" talks about 'falling in love with strangers?'
9. From "Cold As You": "You put up walls and paint them all a shade of ___." What color completes the line?
10. Mine: "Braced myself for the ___, cause that's all I've ever known." "Back to December": "You gave me all your love and all I gave you was ___." What word goes in the blank?

ANSWERS QUIZ 65

1. hospital
2. Should've Said No
3. The Last Time
4. All You Had To Do Was Stay
5. New Romantics
6. 13-Dec-89
7. Smile
8. 22
9. gray
10. goodbye

QUIZ 66

1. Fill in the blank. "I guess _____ really did it this time."
2. Your little hands wrapped around my finger... This first line comes from which song?
3. Turned the lock and put my headphones on, he always said he didn't get this song, but I do, I do. What song is this?
4. We Are Never Ever Getting Back Together is about Taylor Swift and some guy. Why is that Taylor never wants to get back together with him... Like ever?
5. That you were Romeo you were throwing pebbles and my daddy said stay away from Juliet What song?
6. What song are these lyrics from? "So I'll go sit on the floor wearing your clothes. All that I know is I don't know, how to be something you miss."
7. Which recording label released Taylor Swift's first three albums?
8. He is sensible and so incredible and all my single friends are jealous. What song is this from?
9. Does Taylor Swift play any other instruments other than the guitar?
10. What song does this lyric belong to? "I'm sick and tired of your reasons"?

ANSWERS QUIZ 66

1. you
2. Never Grow Up
3. Begin Again
4. Because they fight and then break up and calls her and says "I love you."
5. Love Story
6. Last Kiss
7. Big Machine
8. The Way I Loved You
9. Yes, Piano, Ukulele and Banjo
10. Tell Me Why

QUIZ 67

1. From "Tim McGraw": "Think of my head on your chest and my old _____ blue jeans." Finish this lyric.
2. What song did Taylor Swift sing with Miley Cyrus at the 2009 Grammy Award Show?
3. It's ___ a.m., Feelin' like I just lost a friend. What number goes in the blank from "Breathe"?
4. Which song is this? "We small talk, work and the weather".
5. Charmed?
6. Take me back when our world was one block wide I dared you to kiss me and ran when you tried. Pick the song with these lines.
7. 'Your eyes whispered "___"'. What word finishes the verse?
8. How old was Taylor when she got hired by Sony/ATV Tree publishing house?
9. In 'Dear John', Taylor thinks she is too young to what?
10. Sparks Fly is another track from the album "Speak Now". Fill in the missing word: "Meet me in the pouring rain, kiss me on the ___".

ANSWERS QUIZ 67

1. faded
2. Fifteen
3. two
4. Back to December
5. enchanted
6. Mary's Song (Oh My My My)
7. Have we met?
8. 14
9. be messed with
10. sidewalk

QUIZ 68

1. In what season does the song "Better Than Revenge" begin?
2. Now I'm standing alone in a crowded room and we're not speaking, And I'm dying to know is it killing you like it's killing me, yeah. Which of these is it?
3. In which song does she want to dance in the middle of the parking lot?
4. Which actor from the 'Twilight' movies did Taylor start publicly dating in 2009?
5. In the song "The Outside", where has she never been?
6. Who directed most of Taylor Swift's music videos for her first two albums?
7. What is the name of the song these lyrics go to? "So how could I ever try to be better? When nobody ever lets me in, And I can still see you; this ain't the best view."
8. Which of these songs does NOT have the word "radio" in its lyrics?
9. What fits in the blank from "Tim McGraw"? "When you think Tim McGraw, I hope ___"
10. The Number After Fourteen?

ANSWERS QUIZ 68

1. Summer
2. The Story of Us
3. Fearless
4. Taylor Lautner
5. The outside
6. Trey Fanjoy
7. The Outside
8. Should've Said No
9. you think of me
10. Fifteen

QUIZ 69

1. Did I say something way too honest that made you run and hide like a scared little boy? What song is this lyric from?
2. Which of these is a song about love in the present moment?
3. What song is this from? "Dreaming 'bout the day when you wake up and find that what you're looking for has been here the whole time."
4. Finish the lyric from "You're Not Sorry": "Could've loved you all my life if you hadn't..."
5. Finish the lyric... "So I drive home alone, As I turn out the light, I'll _____"
6. Which one of Taylor's music videos reached number one on CMT's video charts?
7. What song has the lyrics "The smiles the flowers everything is gone"?
8. Fill in the missing word. "State the obvious I didn't get my perfect..."
9. Fill in the blank. "I'll put his _____ down and maybe get some sleep tonight."
10. Finish the lyric from 'Cold As You': "You have a way of..."

ANSWERS QUIZ 69

1. Forever and Always
2. Fearless
3. You Belong with Me
4. left me waiting in the cold
5. put his picture down and maybe get some sleep tonight
6. Tim McGraw
7. Should've Said No
8. fantasy
9. picture
10. coming easily to me

QUIZ 70

1. Which song talks about 'Cory'?
2. I, I loved you in secret/ first sight/ yeah we love without reason Name this song.
3. And baby, for you, I would fall from grace, just to touch your face, if you walk away, I'd beg you on my knees to stay. Which of these songs is correct?
4. From "Come In With The Rain": "But I'll leave my window open, cause I'm too tired at night for all these _____." Which of the following words goes in the blank?
5. Remember when you hit the brakes too soon? twenty stitches in the hospital room, when you started crying, baby, I did, too. Which song is this?
6. It feels like a perfect night to dress up like hipsters, and make fun of our exes. Which song is it?
7. What song does this lyric belong to? "And you got a smile that could light up, this whole town"?
8. From "Enchanted": "There I was again tonight, _____ laughter, _____ smiles." What words complete this line?
9. Finish the line: 'Wearing a gown shaped like a ___.'
10. Your little hand's wrapped around my finger, And it's so quiet in the world tonight, Your little eyelids flutter cause you're dreaming, So I tuck you in, turn on your favorite night light. What song is it?

ANSWERS QUIZ 70

1. Stay Beautiful
2. Dancing With Our Hands Tied
3. Don't Blame Me
4. games
5. Out Of The Woods
6. 22
7. You Belong With Me
8. forcing, faking
9. pastry
10. Never Grow Up

QUIZ 71

1. In "Forever and Always", what type of thing is the singer wondering if she said?
2. Which song contains the lyric: "He is sensible and so incredible"?
3. Which song talks about a guy born on the seventeenth who has his father's eyes?
4. I don't like your little games/ don't like your tilted stage/ the role you made me play What song is this?
5. Flashback when you met me, your buzz cut and my hair bleached, even in my worst times, you could see the best of me. What song is it?
6. From "The Moment I Knew": "And there in the bathroom, I try not to fall apart, and the _____ feeling starts." What word fills in the blank?
7. Say you'll remember me standing in a nice dress, staring at the sunset, babe, red lips and rosy cheeks. What song are these lyrics from?
8. Like oh my, what a marvelous tune, it was the best night, never would forget how he moved. What song is it?
9. What song does this lyric belong to? "You're the only thing I know, like the back of my hand"?
10. From "You Belong With Me": "I'm the one who makes you _____, when you know you're about to cry". What's the missing word?

ANSWERS QUIZ 71

1. Way too honest
2. The Way I Loved You
3. I'd Lie
4. Look What You Made Me Do
5. Dress
6. sinking
7. Wildest Dreams
8. Starlight
9. Breathe
10. laugh

QUIZ 72

1. What kind of an occasion is she barging in on in 'Speak Now'?
2. She looks at life like it's a party and she's on the list, She looks at me like I'm a trend and she's so over it. Which of the following songs is it?
3. Which of these songs does NOT mention pictures in the lyrics?
4. In "The Best Day", what three ages are mentioned?
5. Complete this lyric from "Forever and Always": "Made you run and hide like..."
6. What song talks about taking our love "and tearing it all apart"?
7. It was the best of times/ the worst of crimes/ I struck a match/ it blew your mind are the opening lines from what song?
8. I don't like your kingdom keys, they once belonged to me, you asked me for a place to sleep, locked me out and threw a feast (What?). Which song is this?
9. From "Wildest Dreams": "I thought _____ can't help me now." What word(s) go in the blank?
10. Your kiss, my cheek, I watched you leave, your smile, my ghost, I fell to my knees, when you're young you just run, but you come back to what you need. What song do these lyrics belong to?

ANSWERS QUIZ 72

1. white veil
2. Better Than Revenge
3. Should've Said No
4. 5, 13, and 3
5. a scared little boy
6. A Perfectly Good Heart
7. Getaway Car
8. Look What You Made Me Do
9. heaven
10. This Love

QUIZ 73

1. Photo album on the counter, your cheeks were turning red, you used to be a little kid with glasses in a twin-size bed, your mother's telling stories about you on the tee ball team, you tell me about your past, thinking your future was me. Which of these songs is it?
2. What song does this lyric belong to? "So baby drive slow, 'till we run out of road"?
3. From "Innocent": "Wasn't it easier in your _____ days?" Which of these words goes in the blank?
4. Finish this lyric: 'Where I stand and say ___'?
5. You and I walk a fragile line, I have known it all this time, but I never thought I'd live to see it break. What song is it?
6. A Place In This World: "Maybe I'm just a girl on a mission, but I'm ready to ____". "I'm Only Me When I'm With You": "Don't wanna ____ if you're still on the ground". What word goes in both blank spaces?
7. In "Change", they might be bigger but what are we?
8. Which song has the lyrics "She can't see the way your eyes light up when you smile..."
9. Don't blame me/ love made me crazy/ if it doesn't you ain't doing it right Where do these opening lines come from?
10. Up on the roof with a school girl crush, drinking beer out of plastic cups, say you fancy me, not fancy stuff. What song is it?

ANSWERS QUIZ 73

1. All Too Well
2. Fearless
3. lunchbox
4. Don't say yes run away now
5. Haunted
6. fly
7. Faster and never scared
8. Invisible
9. Don't Blame Me
10. King Of My Heart

QUIZ 74

1. From "Invisible": "She can't see the way your eyes light up when you _____." What word completes the line?
2. Didn't they tell us don't rush into things? didn't you flash your green eyes at me? haven't you heard what becomes of curious minds? What song is it?
3. Before you I'd only dated self-indulgent takers, that took all of their problems out on me. What song is it?
4. What song does this lyric belong to? "As I pace back and forth all this time"?
5. From "Teardrops on My Guitar": "And there he goes, so _____, the kind of _____ I wish I could be". What are the missing words?
6. 'You were in college working part time ___ '. What words complete the line?
7. But now I'll go sit on the floor, Wearing your clothes, All that I know is I don't know, How to be something you miss. What song is it?
8. What two songs have the word scar or scars in the lyrics?
9. How many songs on "Fearless" were written by Taylor herself?
10. What song contains the lyric: "These walls that they put up to hold us back will fall down"?

ANSWERS QUIZ 74

1. smile
2. Wonderland
3. Stay Stay Stay
4. White Horse
5. perfectly, flawless
6. waiting tables
7. Last Kiss
8. Cold As You and "A Perfectly Good Heart"
9. 7
10. Change

QUIZ 75

1. What song has the lyrics "X is the shape I drew through your face.."
2. I wanna be your end game/ I wanna be your first string/ I wanna be your a-team Which song is this?
3. You should take it as a compliment, that I'm talking to everyone here but you. What song is it?
4. From "22": "It feels like a perfect night to dress up like _____." What word completes the lyric?
5. Cause you got that James Dean daydream look in your eye, and I got that red lip classic thing that you like. What upbeat song is this?
6. I was reminiscing just the other day, while having coffee all alone and Lord, it took me away, back to a first-glance feeling on New York time, back when you fit in my poems like a perfect rhyme.
7. What song does this lyric belong to? "Breaking down, and coming undone"?
8. From "Love Story": "We were both young, when I first _____ you". What goes in the blank?
9. 'I was the flight risk with a fear of ___'. What word is missing?
10. In how many songs on Taylor Swift's first two CDs is a car, a car part, or driving mentioned in the lyrics?

ANSWERS QUIZ 75

1. Permanent Marker
2. End Game
3. Gorgeous
4. hipsters
5. Style
6. Holy Ground
7. The Way I Loved You
8. saw
9. falling
10. Eleven

QUIZ 76

1. Who helped write (and provided background vocals for) "Breathe"?
2. What song has the lyrics "and sometimes we don't say a thing just listen to the crickets sing"?
3. What day and time occur in some of Taylor's songs on her album "Fearless"?
4. What's the "first" in the song "Fearless"?
5. What, in "Love Story", does Taylor compare herself to?
6. What song starts out with "Once upon a time"?
7. What song contains the lyric: "They're dimming the street lights"?
8. What guy names are mentioned in this CD?
9. How many songs did Taylor write ALL by herself on this album?
10. Which song mentions short skirts, T-shirts, high heels, and sneakers?

ANSWERS QUIZ 76

1. Colbie Caillat
2. I'm Only Me When I'm With You
3. 2am and Tuesday
4. kiss
5. Juliet and Scarlet Letter
6. Forever and Always
7. Hey Stephen
8. Stephen and Romeo
9. 7
10. You Belong With Me

CPSIA information can be obtained
at www.ICGtesting.com
Printed in the USA
LVHW080518181121
703677LV00015B/592